INTELLIGENCE UNLEASHED

UNDERSTANDING AND HARNESSING THE POWER OF ARTIFICIAL INTELLIGENCE

MARIA FAYAZ

This book is dedicated with all my heart to my parents, teachers, and principal ma'am, Ms. Shobhna Sirohi

Contents

Preface

Artificial Intelligence (AI) seems the defining technology of our time. The first thing that comes to most people's minds when they hear the word artificial intelligence is typically robots. That's because high-profile movies and books frequently include human-like machines that bring havoc on Earth. However nothing could be further from the truth.

Artificial intelligence is founded on the idea that human intelligence can be described in a way that makes it simple for a computer to duplicate it and carry out activities of any complexity. Artificial intelligence aims to emulate cognitive processes in humans. When it comes to concretely defining processes like learning, reasoning, and perception, researchers and developers in the field are making unexpectedly quick progress. Some people think that soon inventors might be able to create systems that are better than what humans are currently capable of learning or understanding. Others, however, continue to hold this view because all cognitive processes involve value judgements that are influenced by human experience.

Artificial intelligence (AI) has captivated the imaginations of scientists, writers, and the general public for decades. From the early days of science fiction to the present, AI has been depicted as both a revolutionary technology and a potential threat. But what is AI, really? And what can it do today?

In this book, we'll explore the complete history of AI, from its origins in ancient mythology to the modern-day algorithms that power everything from self-driving cars to virtual assistants. We'll also delve into the many ways AI is being used in fields such as healthcare, agriculture, and cyber-security, and we'll discuss the myths and realities surrounding AI's capabilities and limitations.

Throughout our journey, we'll ask important questions about the future of AI and what it means for humanity. Will AI eventually surpass human intelligence? Will it lead to a utopian future or a dystopian one? These are just a few of the topics we'll explore as we seek to understand the full potential and implications of this transformative technology.

Acknowledgements

First and foremost, I would like to express my gratitude to my teachers, Mr. Jeelani Karim and Mr. Touseef ibn Farooq. Your insights, encouragement, and guidance were invaluable to me as I worked on this book.

I would also like to thank my parents. I cannot thank you enough for your unwavering support and encouragement throughout my writing journey. Your belief in me and your constant encouragement have meant more to me than I can express. Thank you for always being there for me, and for being such a vital part of my life.

And to Principal Ma'am,

Thank you for your guidance and support over the year. Your wisdom and leadership have been an inspiration to me, and I am grateful for the opportunities you have provided. Your belief in my potential has meant a great deal to me, and I am forever grateful for your guidance and support.

Your support has been essential in helping me to complete this project.

Finally, I want to thank the readers of this book. Your interest in AI and your willingness to learn more about this exciting field are what make all of this work worthwhile. I hope that you will find this book to be a useful and engaging introduction to Artificial Intelligence and that it will inspire you to explore this fascinating field further.

CHAPTER ONE

WHAT IS AI?

Artificial intelligence is a technique for teaching a computer, a robot operated by a computer, or software to think critically and creatively like a human mind. AI is achieved through examining the cognitive process and researching the patterns of the human brain. These research projects produce systems and software that are intelligent.

AI is a topic that, in its most basic form, combines computer science and substantial datasets to facilitate problem-solving. Additionally, it includes the branches of artificial intelligence known as deep learning and machine learning, which are commonly addressed together. These fields use AI algorithms to build expert systems that make predictions or categorise information based on incoming data.

The powers of the human mind can be modelled and even improved upon by machines thanks to artificial intelligence. AI is becoming more and more prevalent in daily life, from the emergence of self-driving cars to the proliferation of smart assistants like Siri and Alexa. As a result, numerous IT firms from a variety of sectors are making investments in artificial intelligence technologies.

The term is frequently used synonymously with its subfields, such as deep learning and machine learning. But there are differences. For instance, machine learning focuses on creating systems that develop new skills or enhance existing ones based on the data they ingest. It's important to note that although all machine learning is AI, not all AI is machine learning.

WEAK AI

Nowadays, artificial intelligence (AI) is typically used to describe weak AI. The only AI now in use, often known as narrow AI, is this one. Although weak AI can do activities faster than humans and tackle complex problems, its skills are constrained by its programming. Despite its name indicating constraint, weak AI permeates many parts of our jobs, personal lives, and entertainment. Weak artificial intelligence (weak AI) is a research and development approach to AI that recognises that computers can only mimic human cognitive function and cannot be aware in any meaningful way. Weak AI is incapable of breaking the rules; it just obeys them and is constrained by them. A good example of weak AI is a character in a computer game who can only act genuinely within the confines of their game character.

Narrow AI is another name for weak AI. Inferring that their responses are frequently pre-programmed, voice-based personal assistants like Siri and Alexa, for instance, could be considered weak AI systems because they only perform a small number of pre-defined functions.

Weak AI does not have high hopes for the outcomes of AI; it only holds that intelligent behaviour can be represented and used by machines to complete difficult jobs and difficulties. But just because a computer exhibits intelligent behaviour does not imply that it has the same level of intelligence as a person. Weak AI helps turn huge amounts of data into useful knowledge by identifying patterns and generating predictions.

Examples of weak AI include the newsfeed on Meta (formerly Facebook), Amazon's suggested purchases, and Apple's Siri, the feature on the iPhone that responds to spoken requests.

One of the problems of weak AI, aside from its constrained capabilities, is the danger of harm if the system malfunctions. Think about an autonomous car that miscalculates the distance to an approaching vehicle, causing a tragic collision.

Strong AI

Artificial general intelligence (AGI), usually referred to as strong artificial intelligence (AI), or general AI, is a theoretical term describing an approach to developing AI. Strong AI would require a machine with an intelligence comparable to humans, a self-aware consciousness, and the capacity to solve problems, learn, and make plans for the future. Indistinguishable from the human mind intelligent machines are what strong AI aspires to build. But just like a child, the AI system would have to learn from its experiences and input, gradually improving and expanding its skills. Strong artificial intelligence is less of an actual method for developing AI and more of a concept. It is a different perspective on AI because it compares it to humans.

It says that a computer may be taught to behave exactly like a human mind, to be intelligent in all senses, to have perception, beliefs, and other cognitive processes that are typically solely attributed to humans. It is nonetheless highly challenging to provide a clear criterion as to what would constitute as a success in the development of strong artificial intelligence because humans cannot even adequately describe what intelligence is. The immediate uses of Applied AI, which produces more observable and quantitative benefits, currently overshadow Strong AI development. Additionally, advancements in embodied systems have not gone beyond the most fundamental building blocks that lack even a cockroach's level of general intelligence. However, it might be claimed that the absence of a concept of intelligence is the single biggest obstacle to Strong AI. (Copeland) There is no universal metric of "success" in the field of strong artificial intelligence because the ultimate goal is to create an intelligent computer that can think and understand, but both concepts remain ambiguous and indefinable.

CHAPTER TWO

HISTORY OF AI

The concept of artificial intelligence, mechanical men, and other automatons existing or having the potential to exist was first raised by thinkers in antiquity, which is when artificial intelligence first emerged.

Throughout the 1700s and beyond, early thinkers helped artificial intelligence become more real. Philosophers wondered whether it was possible to artificially automate and control non-human machine intelligence. Classical philosophers, mathematicians, and logicians first investigated the mechanical manipulation of symbols, which eventually sparked interest in AI and led to the development of the Atanasoff Berry Computer (ABC), the first programmable digital computer, in the 1940s. The development of an "electronic brain" or artificially intelligent entity was spurred forward by this particular invention.

Before AI icons contributed to our current understanding of the topic, about ten years had passed. Alan Turing, a mathematician among other things, created a test that determined how well a machine could mimic human behaviour. The phrase "artificial intelligence" was first used by computer and cognitive scientist John McCarthy in the middle of that decade during a summer conference held at Dartmouth College.

Many researchers, programmers, logicians, and theorists contributed to the development of the current understanding of artificial intelligence as a whole starting in the 1950s. Every decade brought new discoveries and developments that altered people's fundamental understanding of the area of artificial intelligence and how historical advancements have propelled it forward.

Defining Moments in the History of Artificial Intelligence

It's not unexpected that interest in artificial intelligence increased significantly around 1900, but it is remarkable how many people had ideas for AI hundreds of years before there was a term to express what they were considering.

AI between 380 BC and 1900

Between 380 BC to the late 1600s, a variety of mathematicians, theologians, philosophers, professors, and authors pondered the employment of mechanical methods, calculating devices, and numeral systems, which ultimately gave rise to the idea of mechanised "human" thought in non-human entities.

Early 1700s: *Popular literature more frequently featured depictions of all-knowing devices similar to computers. One of the earliest allusions to contemporary technology, specifically a computer, was made in Jonathan Swift's book "Gulliver's Travels" in reference to a contraption called the engine. With the aid and expertise of a non-human intellect, this technology was designed to advance knowledge and mechanical abilities to the point that even the least talented person would appear to be adept (mimicking artificial intelligence.)*

The novel "Erewhon" by author Samuel Butler explored the notion that machines might one day be capable of having consciousness in the year **1872.**

From 1900 to 1950

The speed of invention in artificial intelligence increased significantly as the 1900s arrived.

In **1921,** *the science fiction drama "Rossum's Universal Robots" by Czech writer Karel Apek was published (English translat6r5ion). The first recorded use of the term "robot" was in his play, which addressed the idea of man-made artificial beings. From that moment forward, people adopted the concept of the "robot" and applied it to their studies, creations, and discoveries.*

Fritz Lang's science fiction movie Metropolis from **1927** *depicted a robotic female that was physically identical to the human counterpart from which it drew its likeness. The robot-girl makes a town wide attack after that, wreaking devastation on a futuristic Berlin. This movie is important because it features the first on-screen representation of a robot, which served as inspiration for later well-known non-human* *figures like C-P30 in Star Wars.*

*In **1929**, Japanese researcher and biologist Makoto Nishimura invented Gakutensoku, the country's first robot. The phrase "learning from the laws of nature," or "gakutensoku," suggests that the robot's artificially intelligent mind may draw information from both people and the natural world. Its features included altering its facial expressions and moving its hands and head.*

***In 1939** John Vincent Atanasoff (physicist and inventor), alongside his graduate student assistant Clifford Berry, created the Atanasoff-Berry Computer (ABC) with a grant of $650 at Iowa State University. The ABC weighed over 700 pounds and could solve up to 29 simultaneous linear equations.*

***Giant Brains: Or Machines That Think**, written by computer scientist Edmund Berkeley in **1949**, stated that machines are getting better and faster at managing vast volumes of information. He continued by comparing the capabilities of machines to those of the human mind and asserting that "a machine, therefore, can think" if they were built of "hardware and wire instead of flesh and nerves."*

AI in the 1950s

With an increase in research-based results in AI by numerous computer scientists among others, the 1950s proved to be a time when much advancement in the field of artificial intelligence came to fruition.

*The first essay to explain the creation of a chess-playing computer programme was "Programming a Computer for Playing Chess," which was published in **1950** by Claude Shannon, known as the "father of information theory."*

*In **1950**, **Alan Turing** wrote "**Computing Machinery and Intelligence**," which addressed the The Imitation Game dilemma of whether or not computers are capable of thought. This suggestion eventually evolved into **The Turing Test**, which assessed artificial intelligence in machines. Turing's research examined a machine's capacity for human-like thought. The philosophy of artificial intelligence, which analyses intelligence, consciousness, and ability in machines, has made significant use of the Turing Test.*

*Computer scientist **Arthur Samuel** created the first software to teach itself how to play a game in **1952** when he created a computer programme that could play checkers.*

1955 *saw the creation of a proposal for a workshop on "artificial intelligence" by John McCarthy and a group of colleagues. McCarthy was credited with the official invention of the word in 1956, the year the workshop was held.*

*The first artificial intelligence computer program, Logic Theorist, was created in **1955** by researcher Allen Newell, Herbert Simon, and Cliff Shaw.*

1958: *McCarthy developed Lisp, the most popular and still favoured programming language for artificial intelligence research.*

1959: *Samuel coined the term "machine learning" when speaking about programming a computer to play a game of chess better than the human who wrote its program.*

AI in the 1960s

Through the 1960s, innovation in the field of artificial intelligence increased quickly. The development of new programming languages, the development of robots and automatons, academic study, and the popularity of movies that featured artificially intelligent entities all rose. The significance of AI in the latter part of the 20ᵗʰ century was amply illustrated by this.

__1961__: In New Jersey, __Unimate,__ the industrial robot, created by __George Devol__ in the __1950s__, was the first to work on a General motors assembly line. Transporting die castings from the assembly line and attaching the components to cars were among its duties, which were deemed hazardous for humans to perform.

The symbolic integration issue in freshmen calculus was the topic of the heuristic problem-solving program __SAINT__, which was created in __1961__ by computer scientist and __Professor James Slagle.__

In __1964__, computer scientist __Daniel Bobrow__ developed STUDENT, a pioneering AI system that could handle algebraic word problems. One early achievement in AI natural language processing is STUDENT.

*In **1965**, computer scientist and Professor Joseph Weizenbaum created **ELIZA**, an interactive computer program that could actually have a conversation with a person in English. Weizenbaum wanted to show that communication between a machine and a human mind was "superficial," but he found that a lot of individuals thought ELIZA had anthropomorphic traits.*

***Shakey**, the Robot, commonly known as the **"first electronic person**," was created in **1966** by **Charles Rosen** with the assistance of 11 other people.*

*The sci-fi movie from **1968**, the Stanley Kubrick film: **A Space Odyssey** is released. It includes the sentient computer **HAL** (Heuristically designed Algorithmic computer). Until a malfunction alters HAL's interactions negatively, HAL operates the spacecraft's systems and communicates with the crew as though HAL were a human.*

*Terry Winograd, a professor of computer science, developed the first natural language computer program **SHRDLU** in **1968.***

AI in the 1970s

Similar to the 1960s, the 1970s saw rapid improvements, with a special emphasis on robotics and automatons. However, there were obstacles to artificial intelligence in the 1970s, such as reduced government support for AI research.

***1970: Waseda University** in Japan created **WABOT-1**, the first anthropomorphic robot. Moveable limbs, sight, and communication abilities were among its qualities.*

*In **1973, James Lighthill,** an applied mathematician, gave a report on the state of AI research to the British Science Council, concluding that "in no part of the field have discoveries made so far produced the major impact that was then promised." As a result, the British government drastically reduced support for AI research.*

1977: *The movie **Star Wars**, directed by George Lucas, is released. The humanoid robot C-3PO, a protocol droid who is "fluent in more than seven million kinds of communication," is featured in the movie. In addition to C-3PO, the movie also has R2-D2, a little astromech droid that can only speak through electronic beeps (the opposite of C-3PO). It can co-pilot star fighters and do minor repairs.*

*In **1979, James L. Adams**, a graduate student in mechanical engineering at the time, built **the Stanford Cart**, a remote-controlled, television-equipped mobile robot, in 1961. **Hans Moravec**, a PhD candidate at the time, devised a "slider," or mechanical swivel, that allowed the TV camera to pan side to side in 1979. The cart, one of the earliest demonstrations of an autonomous vehicle, travelled a room full of chairs successfully without human intervention in around five hours.*

AI in the 1980s

Through the 1980s, artificial intelligence continued to advance quickly. Despite developments and enthusiasm surrounding AI, there was worry surrounding an impending "AI Winter," a time of decreased investment and interest in the field.

WABOT-2 *was constructed at Waseda University in* ***1980***. *The WABOT's first iteration gave the humanoid the ability to converse with people, read music scores, and play an electronic organ.*

1981*: **The Fifth Generation Computer project** was funded with $850 million by the Japanese Ministry of International Trade and Industry. Its objective was to create machines that could communicate, translate languages, decipher visual data, and demonstrate human-like reasoning.*

1984 *saw the debut of Steve Barron's film **Electric Dreams**. The story centres on a love triangle between a man, a woman, and "Edgar," a sentient personal computer.*

1984*: At the Association for the Advancement of Artificial Intelligence (AAAI), cognitive scientist **Marvin Minsky** and AI theorist **Roger***

Schank issue a dire warning about the AI winter, the first period of declining support for artificial intelligence research. Within three years, their prophecy came true.

Under the guidance of **Ernst Dickmanns** in **1986**, Mercedes-Benz created and unveiled an autonomous van equipped with cameras and sensors. On a route with no other obstructions and no human drivers, it was able to travel at speeds of up to 55 mph.

Judea Pearl, a philosopher and computer scientist, published "**Probabilistic Reasoning in Intelligent Systems**" in **1988**. **Bayesian networks**, a "probabilistic graphical model" that represents sets of variables and their dependencies via **directed acyclic graph (DAG)** was also invented by him.

In **1988, Rollo Carpenter**, programmer and inventor of two chatbots, **Jabberwacky** and **Cleverbot** (released in the 1990s), developed Jabberwacky to "simulate natural human chat in an interesting, entertaining and humorous manner." This is an example of AI via a chatbot communicating with people.

AI in the 1990s

The end of the millennium was on the horizon, but this anticipation only helped artificial intelligence in its continued stages of growth.

*In **1995**, computer scientist **Richard Wallace** used Weizenbaum's ELIZA as inspiration to create the chatbot **A.L.I.C.E** (Artificial Linguistic Internet Computer Entity). A.L.I.C.E. differed from ELIZA in that it also collected natural language sample data.*

***Recurrent neural network (RNN)** architecture known as **Long Short-Term Memory (LSTM)** was created by computer scientists **Sepp Hochreiter and Jürgen Schmidhuber** in **1997**, which was used for speech and handwriting recognition.*

*In **1997**, IBM's Deep Blue chess-playing computer became the first one to defeat a reigning world champion in a game of chess.*

Furby,** the first robotic "pet" toy for kids, was created in **1998** by **Dave Hampton** and **Caleb Chung.

In **1999**, Sony released **AIBO (Artificial Intelligence RoBOt)**, a $2,000 robotic pet dog designed to "learn" through interacting with its surroundings, owners, and other AIBOs. Its capabilities included the capacity to converse with its human user and comprehend more than 100 voice instructions.

AI from 2000-2010

Following the Y2K scare, AI continued to grow as the new millennium got under way. As predicted, more artificial intelligences were produced, along with imaginative media (particularly film) that explored the idea of AI and its potential future.

The year 2000 problem, sometimes referred to as the Y2K problem, was a class of computer bugs affecting the formatting and storing of electronic calendar data starting on January 1, 2000. Some systems would have problems adjusting to the new year format of 2000 because all internet software and programmes were developed in the 1900s (and beyond). It was a problem for technology and individuals who utilised it because previously, these automated systems merely had to modify the last two digits of the year.

Kismet *was a robot created in 2000 by* **Professor Cynthia Breazeal** *that could understand and mimic emotions through facial expressions. It had features like eyes, lips, eyelids, and eyebrows, just like a human face.*

In **2000,** *Honda unveils* **ASIMO,** *artificially intelligent humanoid robot.*

In **2001** *Sci-fi film A.I. Artificial Intelligence, directed by Steven Spielberg, is released. The movie is set in a futuristic, dystopian society and follows David, an advanced humanoid child that is programmed with anthropomorphic feelings, including the ability to love.*

In **2002**, i-Robot released **Roomba,** an autonomous robot vacuum that cleans while avoiding obstacles.

2004: Without human assistance, NASA's robotic exploration rovers Spirit and Opportunity move over Mars' surface.

Science fiction film I, **Robot** was released by Alex Proyas' in 2004. Humanoid robots serve humanity in the year 2035, but one person is strongly anti-robot as a result of a personal tragedy (determined by a robot.)

The phrase "machine reading" was first used in 2006 by computer scientists Michael Cafarella, Michele Banko, and computer science professor Oren Etzioni to define it as unsupervised autonomous understanding of text.

2007 saw the creation of ImageNet by computer science professor Fei Fei Li and her team. This database of annotated photos serves as a resource for the development of object recognition software.

*Google secretly developed a driverless car in **2004**. It passed Nevada's self-driving test in 2014.*

AI from 2010 to present-day

The last ten years have been crucial for the advancement of AI. Since 2010, artificial intelligence has permeated every aspect of our daily lives. We use computers with "intelligence" features that most of us take for granted and voice assistants on our smartphones. AI is no longer and hasn't been a dream for a while.

The ImageNet Large Scale Visual Recognition Challenge (ILSVRC), *their yearly AI object recognition challenge, was introduced in **2010**.*

***2010** also saw the release of **Microsoft's Kinect** for Xbox 360, the first gaming system to use a 3D camera and infrared detection to track player movement.*

*2011 saw Ken Jennings and Brad Rutter, two previous Jeopardy champions, lose to **Watson**, a natural language question-answering* *computer created by IBM.*

Siri, *a virtual assistant for Apple iOS operating systems, was introduced in* **2011.** *In order to infer, observe, respond to, and recommend things to a human user, Siri uses a natural-language user interface. It responds to voice instructions and offers each user a "individualised experience."*

In **2012***, Google researchers* **Jeff Dean** *and* **Andrew Ng** *taught a huge neural network with 16,000 processors to identify photographs of cats while not providing any more context. They did this by exposing the network to 10 million unlabelled images from YouTube videos.*

Never Ending Image Learner (NEIL), *a semantic machine learning system that could compare and evaluate image associations, was published in* **2013** *by a research team from Carnegie Mellon University.*

In **2014,** *Microsoft launched* **Cortana,** *their version of the iOS virtual assistant Siri.*

2014 *also saw the creation of **Amazon Alexa**, a home assistant that evolved into smart speakers that functions as personal assistants.*

2015 *saw the signing of an open letter prohibiting the development and use of autonomous weapons by Elon Musk, Steve Wozniak, Stephen Hawking, and 3,000 other individuals (for purposes of war.)*

***AlphaGo**, a computer programme that plays the board game Go, defeated a number of (human) champions **between 2015 and 2017**.*

*In **2016, Hanson Robotics** develops **Sophia**, a humanoid robot. She is regarded as the first "citizen robot." Sophia stands out from earlier humanoids due to her resemblance to a real person and her AI-enabled facial emotions, picture recognition, and communication skills.*

*Google announced **Google Home** in **2016,** a smart speaker that employs artificial intelligence to serve as a user's "personal assistant" to help them remember tasks, schedule appointments, and do voice searches for information.*

2017: *To learn how to negotiate, the **Facebook Artificial Intelligence Research lab** taught two "dialogue agents" (chatbots) to talk with one another. The chatbots, which were initially created in English, started to speak in their own language as they talked to one another, showing a strong level of artificial intelligence.*

*In a Stanford reading and comprehension test from **2018**, **Alibaba** (a Chinese tech company languag processing AI outperformed human intelligence. Alibaba's language processing came in with a score of "82.44 against 82.30 on a set of 100,000 questions," – a narrow defeat, but a defeat nonetheless.*

*The first "bidirectional, unsupervised language representation that may be employed on a range of natural language tasks utilising transfer learning" was created by Google in **2018** and is called **BERT**.*

*In **2018**, Samsung unveiled the virtual assistant **Bixby**. Three of Bixby's features are **Voice, Vision**, and **Home**. Voice allows the user to speak to Bixby and ask questions, make recommendations, and make suggestions. Vision uses the camera app to see what the user sees and home, where Bixby makes use of app-based data to assist the user and engage with them (e.g. weather and fitness applications.)*

Artificial intelligence (AI) has worked its way into every aspect of our life during the past several years. We can use complex AI models to tackle the most challenging problems due to techniques like deep learning. However, while people who work in professions that are primarily based on technology are aware of AI's explosive powers, the general public is still mostly unaware of the depth of AI's potential. The development of artificial intelligence is advancing at an unprecedented rate. Therefore, we may anticipate that in the upcoming years, the positive patterns from the past decades will continue.

WHAT CAN AL I DO?

There are so many applications of AI in so many subfields; it is challenging to provide a succinct response. Here are a few examples;

Read

SummarizeBot is an AI-powered programme. Automatic text summarising by artificial intelligence and machine learning reads communication from a variety of sources, including news articles, web links, books, emails, legal documents, audio and image files, and more, and gives back the crucial details. Using blockchain, artificial intelligence, machine learning, and natural language processing, SummarizeBot can now be utilised in Facebook Messenger or Slack.

Write

The ability of artificial intelligence (AI) to produce text that resembles human speech has advanced dramatically in recent years. As a result, corporations and organisations are employing AI writing more frequently to produce everything from financial reports to marketing content. For the purpose of creating their social media postings, several marketers are using artificial intelligence. Artificial intelligence has even produced a novel that was nominated for an award.

See

When a computer is able to "see" the world, interpret visual input, and make judgements about it, this is called machine vision. Machine vision is employed in a variety of remarkable applications today, such as enabling self-driving cars, facial recognition for law enforcement, payment portals, and more. The ability of machines to see in manufacturing aids in preventative maintenance and product quality assurance.

Hear and understand

Artificial intelligence has the capacity to recognise gunshots, evaluate the sound, and then notify the appropriate authorities. One of the astounding things that AI can accomplish when it hears and comprehends noises is this. And who can deny that digital voice assistants are useful for answering your questions, whether you want a weather report or your day's schedule? Business executives adore the ease, effectiveness, and accuracy that AI's automatic meeting minutes offer.

Speak

Speaking is a capability of artificial intelligence. While having Alexa and Google

Maps react to your questions and provide directions is beneficial (and entertaining), Google Duplex goes one step further by utilising AI to make appointments and carry out chores over the phone in a highly conversational manner. It is also capable of accurately responding to responses made by the people it is speaking to.

Smell

researchers working on artificial intelligence are creating models that will be able to identify diseases simply by sniffing a person's breath. In addition to cancer, diabetes, and brain traumas, it can also detect the "woody, musky odour" released by Parkinson's disease before any other symptoms are recognised. These compounds, known as aldehydes, are linked to human illnesses and stress. Bots with artificial intelligence might also detect gas leaks or other caustic chemicals. IBM is even developing new scents with AI.

Touch

In order to help robots grab and recognise items more readily, MIT researchers introduced an artificial intelligence (AI) system that can visualise by touching and feel by perceiving. While the physical world can be felt through our sense of touch, our eyes enable us to quickly comprehend the whole context of these tactile messages. Robots that have been programmed to see or feel are not quite as interchangeable with these signals. A robot that can recognise "supermarket ripe" raspberries using sensors and cameras and can even pick them up and put them in a basket! Linking touch with other senses is the next step in the development of tactile AI.

Move

All kind of movement, including that of robots, drones, and autonomous vehicles, is propelled by artificial intelligence. The Alter 3 production at Tokyo's New National Theatre features robots that can generate motion autonomously.

Understand emotions

AI systems that monitor a person's emotions as they view videos are helping market research. Artificial emotional intelligence can acquire information from a person's body language, facial expressions, and other cues, compare it to an emotion database to ascertain what emotion is probably being exhibited, and then decide on an action based on that information.

Play games

Artificial intelligence isn't all serious business—it can master games like chess, go, and poker (which was a remarkable achievement)! And it turns out that AI is capable of mastering these games, competing with humans, and even winning!

Debate

IBM's Project Debater demonstrated to us that artificial intelligence is even capable of winning human debates on challenging topics. In addition to researching a subject, it can also develop a compelling point of view and write rebuttals for a human opponent. In Israel's Haifa, Project Debater was created at an IBM lab. Noam Slonim put forth the project as the next IBM Research Grand Challenge in 2011, following Deep Blue and Watson's triumph on Jeopardy! It was originally made public on June 18, 2018, in San Francisco during a closed media event led by Slonim and Ranit Aharonov, both of the IBM Research lab in Haifa, Israel.

Noa Ovadia, the Israeli debate champion from 2016, and Dan Zafrir competed against the AI technology. The two had a discussion on the topics "we should subsidise space exploration" and "Should we increase the use of telemedicine.

Create

Even the creative processes of creating visual art, poetry, music, and pictures can be mastered by artificial intelligence. Even Google's AI was able to produce an AI "kid" that performed better than human-made substitutes. Typically, a dataset of 5.85 billion images is used to train AI models to produce art. This enormous volume of data is required for the AI to learn about the artistic ideas and image content. Additionally, processing takes a very long period.

Image Recognition

As it is presented to machines for recognition, artificial intelligence (AI) is developing its intellectual capacity. The more extensive and flexible your AI is, the better it will be able to recognise, comprehend, and predict in a wide range of circumstances. Image recognition enables computer vision to precisely identify objects in the world around us. It is impossible to find or identify objects without picture recognition. We must fully comprehend picture recognition since it is crucial to computer vision. The art of recognising and interpreting images with the goal of identifying the objects, places, people, or things seen in one's natural surroundings is known as image recognition, and it is a subfield of computer vision. The primary goal is still to view the items as a human brain would. All of these things are intended to be detected and analysed by image recognition, which then derives conclusions from the analysis. However, the term "computer vision" encompasses a broader range of techniques for obtaining, scrutinising, and processing data from the outside world for use by machines. Similar to how people do it, image recognition analyses each pixel of an image to extract usable information. AI cameras are capable of identifying a variety of objects thanks to computer vision training.

Transcribe speech

As the name implies, AI transcription turns spoken words into text by utilising AI technology. Manual note-taking is no longer necessary. Instead, you can "hire" transcription software to hear conversations or audio or video recordings and convert them into texts without any difficulty.

Translate languages

The process of real-time translation has changed significantly throughout time. Speech would first be converted to text in earlier iterations of this technology before being translated into the target language. Using AI has allowed for additional process improvement. The current real-time translation technology uses sophisticated pattern-matching software that can differentiate noises. It is based on artificial intelligence and several types of machine learning. It uses pattern-matching sound identification software. Neural networks and deep learning programmes are utilised to clearly understand what is being said and to be understood in terms of the context of words and sentences.

Recognise emotions in speech

With the help of text, voice tone, gestures, and facial expressions, emotional AI can understand the emotions of others and modify its behaviour accordingly. Although humans are better at identifying various emotions, AI is catching up with this skill because to its increased capacity for data analysis.

Drive

In the 2005 DARPA Grand Challenge, STANLEY, a driverless robotic automobile, finished the 132-mile course first by travelling at 22 mph through the difficult terrain of the Mojave Desert. In order to perceive its surroundings, STANLEY is a Volkswagen Touareg equipped with cameras, radar, and laser rangefinders. Onboard software controls the vehicle's steering, braking, and acceleration (Thrun, 2006). The next year, CMU's BOSS won the Urban Challenge by driving through the streets of an abandoned Air Force base safely in traffic while adhering to the rules of the road and avoiding other vehicles, people, and other obstacles.

Fly drones

Drones can be managed by AI so they can fly on their own. This makes drones even more adaptable because they can be operated without a human operator. AI can be used to automate drones in a few distinct ways.

Read our mind

The idea of AI having the ability to read minds is quite astounding. It has the ability to decode brain information before producing speech. Impressive and transformative for people who have trouble speaking, but a little unsettling when you take into account the mind-reading component of the skill. It's not surprising that some of the biggest internet companies, like Facebook and Elon Musk, are working on their own initiatives to take advantage of AI's potential for mind-reading. A computer can read your mind with 83% accuracy by scanning your brain and presenting what you're thinking about as visuals. A new AI programme has the ability to read minds. By observing your brain activity, it enables a computer to produce visuals of what you are picturing.

Predict

You engage with artificial intelligence every time you launch Netflix, open Spotify, or visit the "you might also like" area of an e-commerce site. Engines that generate recommendations using machine learning are among the most frequently utilised AI applications today. These engines get better and better at predicting which recommendations you'll like as they gather information about your behaviours.

AI is also capable of forecasting future developments, such as changes to the stock market. Investors can use these forecasts to guide their stock buying and selling decisions. But AI is not infallible. Although their forecasts are based on accurate and reliable data, they sometimes fail to take unexpected events into consideration. As a result, investors should use AI as one of several tools when selecting stocks to buy or sell.

CHAPTER FOUR

AI IN SCIENCE AND HEALTHCARE

The remarkable applications AI could have for the medical industry have only just begun to be explored by AI experts. The medical sciences make substantial use of computer systems with artificial intelligence. Common uses include remote patient treatment, prescription transcription, increasing doctor-patient communication, medication discovery and development from beginning to end, and patient diagnosis. Modern computer algorithms have lately achieved accuracy levels that are comparable to those of human experts in the field of medical sciences, despite the fact that computer systems frequently perform jobs more quickly than humans do. According to others, it won't be long until humans are

entirely replaced in some positions within the medical sciences. Machine learning models are used in medicine to scan medical data and uncover insights to assist enhance patient experiences and health outcomes. Artificial intelligence (AI) has recently made significant strides in computer science and informatics, and it is now becoming a crucial component of contemporary healthcare. Medical practitioners are supported by AI algorithms and other applications powered by AI in clinical settings and current research. Clinical decision assistance and image analysis are currently AI's most prevalent uses in medical settings. By giving them instant access to information or research that is pertinent to their patient, clinical decision support systems assist physicians in making decisions about treatments, drugs, mental health, and other patient requirements. AI technologies are being used to analyse CT scans, x-rays, MRIs, and other pictures in the field of medical imaging in order to look for lesions or other findings that a human radiologist would overlook. AI has many potential benefits for the practise of medicine, like accelerating research or assisting clinicians in making better decisions. Here are some examples of how AI is improving healthcare and Science:

Detect skin cancer:

In order to accurately distinguish between malignant and benign skin lesions, 58 dermatologists from 17 different nations participated in a study that was earlier this year published in the Annals of Oncology. The cancer-detecting AI scored 95%, exceeding its human counterpart in nearly 1 in 10 cases, while the dermatologists in the study accurately recognised the malignant lesions in 86.6% of cases.

Diagnosis of Lung cancer:

According to a recent study from Stanford University, machine learning algorithms can identify tissue slides demonstrating a certain form of cancer with a great deal more accuracy than human epidemiologists. This finding may raise some eyebrows in the medical world. It's one of the first signs that computers aren't simply capable of handling the "subjective" aspects of medicine, but that they're sometimes even more effective at solving these issues than actual doctors.

Viz.ai's *AI-powered healthcare solutions help care teams respond more quickly in the healthcare industry, where delays can mean the difference between life and death. The* *company's AI technologies can immediately identify problems and alert care teams, allowing professionals to evaluate options and make treatment decisions that could save lives.To help pathologists make more precise diagnoses, **PathAI** develops machine learning technology. The company's current objectives include lowering cancer diagnosis inaccuracy and creating strategies for personalised medical care.To bring its AI technology to additional healthcare sectors, PathAI collaborated with companies like Bill & Melinda Gates Foundation and pharmaceutical companies like Bristol-Myers Squibb.*

__Regard__, a firm in the healthtech industry, employs AI to diagnose patients. The automated solution, according to the business, serves as the "clinical co-pilot" for EMRs. To make a diagnosis, the data from EMRs is combined. Additionally, detailed advice regarding patient care are given to healthcare professionals. Additionally, the system automatically updates patient records to lessen healthcare workers' burnout.

An AI-based symptom and cure checker called __Buoy Health__ use algorithms to identify and treat illnesses. The process goes as follows: a chatbot asks a patient about their symptoms and health concerns, then, after making a diagnosis, directs the patient to the appropriate care.A team from Harvard Medical School created Buoy's AI, which aids in quicker patient diagnosis and treatment.

*In order to speed up radiology diagnosis, **Enlitic** creates deep learning medical tools. With the help of the company's deep learning platform, doctors may gain a better understanding of a patient's current needs by analysing unstructured medical data such as radiological pictures, blood tests, EKGs, genomes, and patient medical history.*

*AI is used by **Freenome** in cancer screenings, diagnostic procedures, and blood tests. Freenome seeks to find cancer in its earliest stages and then create novel treatments by implementing AI during routine checkups.*

***Beth Israel Deaconess Medical Center**, a teaching hospital connected with Harvard University, employed AI to make early diagnoses of potentially fatal blood disorders.Doctors created AI-enhanced microscopes to scan blood samples more quickly than is possible with manual screening for dangerous pathogens like E. coli and staphylococcus. To teach the computers how to look for bacteria, the researchers used 25,000* *photos of blood samples. Then, with 95% accuracy, the machines learned to recognise and forecast dangerous germs in blood.*

*In order to improve disease diagnosis and therapy, **Iterative Health** integrates AI with gastroenterology. The company's AI Recruitment service automates the process of selecting people who are qualified to be potential candidates for clinical trials for inflammatory bowel disease.*

Additionally, Iterative Health submitted for FDA review the first clinical study of its SKOUT gadget, a tool that employs AI to assist physicians in finding possibly malignant polyps.

VirtuSense *tracks a patient's movements with AI sensors to alert carers and providers of impending falls. The company's products include VST Balance, which uses AI and machine vision to assess a person's risk of falling within the next year, and VSTAlert, which can anticipate when a patient wants to stand up and inform the necessary medical staff.*

*For early disease detection, **Caption Health** integrates AI and ultrasound technology. AI directs healthcare professionals during the ultrasound procedure in real time, resulting in diagnostic-quality images that the software subsequently aids in interpreting and evaluating.The Bill & Melinda Gates Foundation awarded Caption Health a $4.95 million grant to support the creation of AI-guided lung ultrasound, and the company's platform is already used for cardiac ultrasound pictures.*

*AI is used by **BioXcel Therapeutics** to find and create new drugs in the areas of neurology and immuno-oncology. The business's drug re-innovation initiative also uses AI to uncover fresh uses for current medications or to identify new patients.*

*Pharmaceutical company **Reverie Labs** uses computational chemistry and machine learning methods for medication development. In order to better understand cancer and create successful cancer treatments, it makes use of advanced databases and predictive analytics techniques.*

A clinical-stage AI-based biotech platform called **BERG** *maps diseases to hasten the discovery and creation of ground-breaking medications. BERG creates product candidates to treat uncommon diseases by fusing its "Interrogative Biology" method with conventional research and development.*

XtalPi's ID4 *platform, which combines AI, the cloud, and quantum physics, predicts the chemical and pharmacological properties of potential small-molecule therapeutic candidates. The business also asserts that their crystal structure prediction technology anticipates complicated chemical systems in days as opposed to weeks or months. Investors in XtalPi have included Sequoia Capital, Google, and Tencent.*

Atomwise *employs artificial intelligence to fight deadly diseases like multiple sclerosis and Ebola. Identifying patient features for clinical trials and predicting bioactivity are both assisted by the company's neural network,* **AtomNet**. *According to reports, Atomwise's AI system may produce results 100 times faster than conventional pharmaceutical businesses by screening between 10 and 20 million genetic compounds daily.*

*Researchers can uncover prospects for medications that treat neurodegenerative and neuromuscular disorders using **Deep Genomics'** AI platform. A drug's chances of clearing clinical trials while also shortening the time and cost to market are statistically increased when the correct candidates are identified early in the development process."Project Saturn" from Deep Genomics examines over 69 billion distinct cell molecules and gives researchers feedback.*

***BenevolentAI's** main objective is to deliver the appropriate therapy to the appropriate patients at the appropriate time by utilising AI to improve target selection and offer previously unrecognised insights through deep learning. BenevolentAI collaborates with charities to create medications that are portable and works with large pharmaceutical companies to licence drugs.*

***Iodine Software** is developing AI-powered and machine-learning solutions for mid-revenue cycle leakages, like resource optimization and higher response rates, with the aim of enhancing patient care. The company's CognitiveML software identifies client insights, completes accuracy of documentation, and highlights missing data.*

*In order to offer individuals care within the constraints of their schedules, **Kaia Health** runs a digital therapeutics platform with live physical therapists. For the treatment of chronic back pain and COPD, the platform offers individualised programmes with case studies, workout plans, stress-relieving exercises, and learning resources.A PT-grade automated feedback coach is another element of Kaia Health that makes use of AI technology. Kaia Health is accessible as an employer-sponsored benefit or as an integration with top medical specialists.*

*Employers who want to give their staff the tools to maintain good mental health can use **Spring Health**'s mental health benefit solution. Each person's whole dataset is collected as part of the clinically approved technology's operation, and it is compared to hundreds of thousands of other data points. The software then matches users with the appropriate specialist for in-person care or telemedicine appointments using a machine learning approach.*

Through a combination of IoT technology, AI, data science, medical science, and healthcare, **Twin Health**'s *holistic approach aims to address and maybe repair chronic illnesses like Type 2 Diabetes. A digital representation of human metabolic function based on thousands of health data points, everyday activities, and individual preferences was developed by the business and named the Whole Body Digital Twin. Members can receive individualised nutrition, sleep, movement, and breathing assistance through the company's Twin Service.*

Olive's *AI platform automates routine medical tasks so that administrators can focus on more important ones. To free up staff members to concentrate on patient care, the software automates everything from eligibility checks to unresolved claims and data migrations. Olive's AI as a Service interfaces with the tools and software that a hospital already uses, so there is no need for pricey integrations or downtimes.*

An AI-based software platform called **Qventus** addresses operational issues, such as those involving emergency rooms and patient safety. The company's automated software can map the quickest ambulance routes, manage hospital waiting times, and prioritise patient illness and injuries.

The **ClevelandClinic** and IBM collaborated on the Discovery Accelerator, an AI-infused initiative aimed at accelerating medical advancements.A foundation for research in fields like population health, chemistry and drug discovery, and genomics is being built by the joint centre. To innovate patient care and responses to public health concerns, the collaboration uses big data medical research.

*Together with GE Healthcare, **Johns Hopkins Hospital** is enhancing the effectiveness of patient operational flow by utilising predictive AI techniques.An AI-enhanced task force quickly set patient-centered priorities for hospital work. Since starting the initiative, the facility has been 38% faster at allocating beds to patients who are brought into the emergency department.*

***Babylon** is on a mission to reengineer healthcare by changing the emphasis from treating the ill to preventing illness, which will result in improved health and lower medical costs. The platform includes an AI engine developed by medical professionals and deep learning scientists that runs an interactive symptom checker and uses known symptoms and risk factors to deliver the most accurate and current medical information. The Babylon platform also has a monitoring system to assist people in maintaining their health for extended periods of time.*

*For managing chronic illnesses like diabetes and high blood pressure as well as for controlling weight, **One Drop** offers a discrete solution. With interactive coaching from real-world experts, predictive glucose readings powered by AI and data science, learning resources, and daily tracking of readings taken* *from One Drop's Bluetooth-enabled glucose reader and other devices, the One Drop Premium app empowers people to take control of their conditions.*

*Machine learning is used by **CloudMedX** to produce insights for improving patient journeys across the entire healthcare system.The company's technology uses predictive analytics to intervene at crucial points in the patient care process, assisting hospitals and clinics in managing patient data, clinical history, and payment information. These information can be used by healthcare professionals to move patients through the system quickly.*

*AI is used by **Subtle Medical** to enhance images for radiology departments. The SubtlePET and SubtleMR technologies integrate with existing equipment at a facility to accelerate MRI and PET scans while lowering image noise. Through daily patient scans, the software has the potential to reduce wait times.*

*AI is used by **Happify Health by twill** to provide users with individualised treatment plans. The company creates Sequences that tailor tracks for managing medical diseases including multiple sclerosis and psoriasis using its Intelligent Healing Platform. These* *customised programmes may offer coaching, care communities, and digital treatments.*

IBM's Watson, *a former Jeopardy champion supercomputer, now assists healthcare workers in using their data to boost hospital efficiency, engage patients more effectively, and enhance patient care. Watson uses their expertise to do everything from creating individualized treatment plans to deciphering genetic test results and recognize early disease symptoms.*

In order to customize medical treatments, ***Tempus*** *employs AI to comb through the largest database of clinical and molecular data in the world. The business creates AI technologies that provide doctors with insights into diagnoses and treatments.*

An end-to-end platform called **ClosedLoop.ai** *uses AI to identify at-risk individuals and suggest possible treatments. Healthcare companies can use the platform to collect looping feedback, outreach and engagement initiatives, and digital therapies while also receiving individualised data about the requirements of patients. Healthcare providers, payers, pharma, and life science firms can all use the platform.*

__Beacon Biosignals__' EEG analytics platform, which makes use of portal reporting, standardised neurobiomarkers, and machine learning algorithms that "raise the probability of success at each stage of drug development," intends to cure neurological and psychiatric illnesses. Population stratification is additionally used to identify different patient populations.

Utilizing information from current sources, __KenSci__ uses big data and AI to anticipate clinical, financial, and operational risks. It can predict anything from who might become ill to what is increasing a hospital's healthcare expenditures. The companies GE, KPMG, Allscripts, and Microsoft have all been KenSci partners.

A digital pathology tool called __Proscia__ employs AI to find patterns in cancer cells. The company's software aids pathology labs in removing data management bottlenecks and connects data points to enhance cancer identification and therapy through AI-powered image analysis.

A healthcare system's data is analysed by __H2O.ai__'s AI to mine, automate, and predict processes. It has been applied to forecast ICU transfers, enhance clinical processes, and identify a patient's infection risk in a hospital. Hospitals can forecast and identify sepsis using the company's AI to mine health data, which eventually lowers fatality rates.

*With its Digital Life Platform, **ICarbonX** examines human life features more thoroughly using AI and big data. The company believes its big data will aid in the management of all facets of health by studying the health and behavior of people in a "carbon cloud." ICarbonX is certain that its technology can collect enough information to more accurately categorize symptoms, create treatment choices, and improve people's health.*

***Vicarious Surgical** enables surgeons to do minimally invasive procedures by fusing virtual reality with AI-enabled robotics. The company's technology allows surgeons to virtually shrink and thoroughly examine a patient's inside organs. Former Microsoft CEO Bill Gates invested in Vicarious Surgical due to its technology concept.*

*Utilizing the most recent developments in micro instrumentation, endoscope design, data science, and AI, **Auris Health** creates a variety* *of robots to enhance endoscopies. As a result, doctors have a better understanding of a patient's ailment from both a physical and statistical standpoint. In an effort to one day find a cure for lung cancer, the company is creating AI robots to research the disease.*

The **Accuray CyberKnife** *technology precisely treats malignant tumours by combining AI and robotics. Stereotactic body radiation therapy and stereotactic radiosurgery can now be customized for each patient thanks to technology. Rather than treating the entire body, doctors and surgeons can treat the damaged areas with the robot's real-time tumor-tracking capabilities.*

Intuitive's da Vinci *platforms, the first robotic surgery assistant approved by the FDA, have cameras, robotic arms, and surgical equipment to help with minimally invasive treatments. Da Vinci systems continuously gather data and give surgeons analytics to enhance upcoming surgeries. Over ten million procedures have benefited from Da Vinci's assistance.*

Heartlander *is a little mobile robot created by the Robotics Institute at Carnegie Mellon*

University to help with heart treatment. The tiny robot enters the chest by a tiny incision, travels to specific areas of the heart on its own, clings to the surface of the heart, and delivers therapy under the direction of a doctor.

Microsure *robots assist surgeons in overcoming their physical limitations. The motion stabilizer technology developed by the company is meant to increase functionality and accuracy during surgical procedures. Engineers and surgeons at the company created the MUSA surgical robot, which can be operated using joysticks to perform microsurgery.*

AI is already at work enhancing convenience and efficiency, lowering costs and errors, and generally making it simpler for more patients to access the healthcare they require. Examples include patient self-service, chatbots, computer-aided detection (CAD) systems for diagnosis, and image data analysis to identify candidate molecules in drug discovery. Across industries, artificial intelligence (AI) is revolutionizing how we communicate, consume information, and buy goods and services. AI is already transforming the patient experience, how physicians practice medicine, and how the pharmaceutical sector functions in the field of health care. The journey has just begun and there is so much more to come.

CHAPTER FIVE

AI In The Agricultural Sector

One of the oldest and most significant professions in the world is agriculture and farming. It has a significant impact on the economy. By 2050, the population is predicted to exceed nine billion, necessitating a 70% increase in agricultural output to meet the need. Land, water, and other resources are running out due to the growing world population, making it impossible to maintain the demand-supply cycle. Therefore, we must adopt a wiser strategy, increase our level of efficiency when farming, and strive to maximize our output. Let us know about the difficulties farmers experience while utilizing traditional agricultural techniques as well as how artificial intelligence is revolutionizing the

industry by displacing inefficient traditional techniques with more effective ones and making the world a better place.

Preparing the soil: *Farmers prepare the soil for seeding in this earliest stage of farming. Large soil clumps must be broken up and debris, such as sticks, pebbles, and roots, removed during this procedure. Additionally, depending on the type of crop, add fertilisers and organic materials to the environment to make it appropriate for crops.*

sowing seeds, *it's important to consider the space between each seed and the depth at which to plant them. Climate factors like temperature, humidity, and rainfall are significant at this stage.*

Fertilizer addition: *Maintaining soil fertility is crucial for the farmer to be able to cultivate nourishing and healthy crops. Fertilizers are used by farmers because they provide plant nutrients including nitrogen, phosphorus, and potassium. Fertilizers are simply nutrients that are planted and added to agricultural areas to augment the necessary minerals already present in the soil. This stage affects the crop's quality as well.*

Irrigation: This step aids in maintaining humidity and soil moisture. Crop growth can be hampered by under- or overwatering, and if done improperly, can result in damaged crops.

Protecting against weeds: Weeds are unwelcome plants that sprout up next to crops or along agricultural boundaries. Because weeds reduce yields, raise production costs, interfere with harvest, and degrade crop quality, weed prevention is a crucial consideration.

Harvesting: Gathering mature crops from the fields is the process of harvesting. This activity is labor-intensive because it calls for numerous workers. Additionally, post-harvest processing tasks like cleaning, sorting, packing, and refrigeration are included in this step.

Storage is the stage of the post-harvest system when products are held in order to ensure food security outside of agricultural seasons. Crop packing and transportation are also included.

Listing the broad difficulties that the agricultural sector faces:

1.

In farming, climatic variables including rainfall, temperature, and humidity are crucial to the cycle of agriculture. Farmers find it challenging to make judgements on how to prepare the soil, plant seeds, and harvest as a result of rising deforestation and pollution.

1.

The soil must have a certain level of nutrients for each crop. The three main nutrients that soil needs are nitrogen (N), phosphorus (P), and potassium (K). Poor crop quality may result from nutritional insufficiency.

3.

The agriculture lifecycle shows that weed control is crucial, as can be seen. Unless it is regulated, it can raise production costs and deplete the soil of nutrients by absorbing nutrients from the soil.

In order to improve a wide range of agriculture-related tasks throughout the entire food supply chain, the industry is turning to Artificial Intelligence technologies. These technologies can help produce healthier crops, control pests, monitor soil and growing conditions, organise data for farmers, lessen workloads, and control pests.

Use of weather forecasting: *Farmers find it challenging to determine the best time to plant seeds due to climate change and rising pollution. With the aid of artificial intelligence, however, farmers can analyse weather conditions by using weather forecasting, which aids in planning the type of crop that can be grown and when seeds should be sown.*

Soil and crop health monitoring system: *The kind of soil and nutrition of the soil have a significant impact on the crops that are grown and their quality. The quality of the soil is deteriorating as a result of growing deforestation, making it difficult to assess.*

*An IT startup established in Germany **PEAT** has created an AI-based tool called **Plantix** that can detect nutrient deficits in soil as well as plant pests and illnesses, giving farmers the knowledge they need to utilise fertiliser to increase the quality of their harvest. Utilizing picture recognition-based technology, this app. Smartphones can be used by the farmer to take pictures of the plants. Through short videos on this application, we can also view soil restoration methods with advice and other alternatives.*

In a similar manner, **TraceGenomics** *is another machine learning-based company that aids farmers in doing a soil study. With the aid of these kinds of apps, farmers can monitor the quality of their soil and crops, resulting in healthier, more productive crops.*

Analyzing crop health by drones*: Drone-based Ariel imaging systems from SkySqurrel Technologies have been introduced to monitor crop health. This method uses a drone to collect data from fields, which are subsequently sent by USB drive to a computer for expert analysis. This company analyses the photographs it has collected using algorithms and then provides a thorough report on the state of the farm. It aids in the identification of pests and germs, enabling farmers to utilise pest control measures and other approaches when necessary to take the necessary action.*

Precision farming and predictive analytics *are two examples of how artificial intelligence in agriculture has created tools and applications that assist farmers in conducting accurate and controlled farming by giving them the right guidance regarding water* *management, crop rotation, timely harvesting, the type of crop to be grown, optimal planting, pest attacks, and nutrition management. AI-enabled systems make weather predictions, monitor agricultural sustainability, and assess farms for the presence of diseases or pests and undernourished plants using data like temperature, precipitation, wind speed, and sun radiation in combination with photographs taken by satellites and drones.*

With equipment as basic as an SMS-enabled phone and the Sowing App, farmers without connectivity may profit from AI right away. Farmers with Wi-Fi connectivity can utilise AI apps to get a constantly AI-tailored plan for their farms, in the meantime. Farmers can meet the increased demand for food while growing output and revenues responsibly and without diminishing priceless natural resources with the help of IoT and AI-driven technologies.

AI will assist farmers in the future as they become agricultural technologists, utilising data to maximise yields down to individual plant rows.

Agriculture robots: *AI companies are creating robots that can effortlessly carry out a variety of activities in agricultural settings. When compared to humans, these robots are trained to harvest crops more quickly and in greater quantities while controlling weeds. These robots are taught to harvest and pack crops while simultaneously inspecting the crops' quality and looking for weeds. These robots can also overcome difficulties presented by agricultural forced labour.*

AI-enabled pest detection system: *One of the deadliest enemies of farmers who cause agricultural damage are pests. AI systems employ satellite photos and historical data to determine whether any insects have landed and, if so, which species—such as locusts, grasshoppers, and others—have done so. AI aids farmers in their battle against pests by sending alerts to their smartphones so that farmers may take the necessary precautions* and employ the necessary pest management.

With the aid of artificial intelligence, farmers may automate their operations while also switching to precise cultivation for improved crop quality and production while consuming fewer resources.

Companies working to advance machine learning or AI-based goods and services, such as training data for agriculture, drones, and automated manufacturing, will benefit from future technological advancements that will bring more beneficial applications to this industry, assisting the world in addressing issues related to food production for the expanding population.

HOW AI IS ENHANCING CYBER-SECURITY

A growing number of human information security teams rely on artificial intelligence technologies to aid in their work. Since humans are unable to keep up with the constantly evolving attack surfaces of modern companies, artificial intelligence can now provide the analysis and threat detection that cyber-security professionals need to reduce the risk of a breach and improve the security posture. AI is well-suited to address the world's constantly evolving security concerns because of its adaptability. Companies that store sensitive data can use AI to automate threat detection and stay one step ahead of cybercriminals. AI is used in cyber security to safeguard corporate assets and user data. AI is well-suited for

integration with cyber-security systems due to a number of aspects, including:

Network Traffic Monitoring:

Through an organisation network, businesses and their clients exchange a huge amount of data. Hackers and anyone who wants unwanted access to this confidential data must be avoided. However, IT security experts are unable to impartially assess this traffic.

The Identification of Unknown Threats by AI

Some of a company's risks might be incomprehensible to humans. Every year, hackers launch hundreds of millions of attacks for various reasons. An unidentified threat has the potential to destroy a network completely. The harm they can cause before you catch them is worse.

Vulnerability management:

The best method for protecting a company's network is proper vulnerability management. Given the volume of data that passes through it, this traffic needs to be discovered, identified, and kept out of a company's network.

AI Gets Smarter With Time:

Artificial intelligence technology uses its intelligence to continuously enhance network security. The network's patterns are found and grouped by the algorithm. Then, it looks for security issues and reacts appropriately.

Reduction of Duplicative Processes:

Cybercriminals are constantly searching for new ways to breach corporate networks and take their valuable data. We frequently use the same fundamental security precautions every day. If human security specialists get bored or worn out, your network can be vulnerable to intruders.

Increased Security Generally:

Various threats can be encountered by business networks at any time. Some assaults, including ransomware and denial-of-service attacks, can occur simultaneously. Setting priorities for security responsibilities in a company is difficult as a result.

Improved Endpoint Security:

The number of devices we use at work is growing, making it harder for security experts to stay up. Security on devices is growing more and more dependent on AI. Based on recognised signatures, antivirus software and virtual private networks (VPNs) can defend your computer from malware and ransomware.

A Lot Of Data Can Be Handled by AI:

Company networks are replete with activity. Even in a medium-sized company, there is a lot of traffic. Customers and companies share a large amount of data. This information needs to be protected by both people and software. The volume of traffic that cybersecurity experts can scan has a limit.

Risk Foresight:

AI systems can be used to determine the inventory of your IT assets, both tangible and intangible. Cybercriminals frequently attack these assets. Thanks to AI in cybersecurity, it is now feasible to anticipate how and when a cyberattack will occur and make the necessary preparations to direct resources to the most vulnerable areas.

Authentication Security:

Every day, millions of commercial websites throughout the world request personal information such as usernames, passwords, credit card numbers, and ID images. Organizations require an additional layer of security that safeguards the site's back end in order for this information to be secure.

Artificial intelligence plays a critical role in assisting enterprises in reducing the risk of data breaches and improving their overall cybersecurity posture. In cybersecurity, AI is used to identify patterns and trends in historical data. On the basis of this information, predictions about upcoming assaults can then be made. With AI-powered systems, automatic reactions and quicker cyberthreat eradication are also feasible. Because of the expansion and evolution of the corporate attack surface, cyber threats and attacks are no longer a human-scale issue. The amount of time-varying signals that must be examined in order to effectively measure risk might vary greatly depending on the size of the organisation.

CAN AI BE CREATIVE?

We all recognise creativity when we see it, even if there is no universal description of it, just as there is no global definition of love. Can a computer recognize creativity, then? What's more, can we train a computer to be imaginative? Recent AI developments seem to indicate that the answers are unambiguous "yes."

No one is born with skills like writing, drawing, or singing; instead, we acquire them via observation and application of information, a process we refer to as "learning."

Similar to humans, AI may observe and learn from data to develop creative abilities such as sketching, writing, and musical composition. The gold standard for AI is machine learning, which entails swiftly and effectively training an AI model on much more data than a human could consume in a lifetime, whether that data is text, music, photos, or other types of data.

The theory goes that if you feed AI 100,000 poems or 1 million pieces of pop music, the AI can analyze the patterns in them and then come up with its own. So today, AI has been used in a number of creative fields traditionally assumed to be "uniquely human".

AI creating Art

For two recent examples, the AI-created Portrait of Edmond Belamy sold for almost $430,000, and Sophia, a robot, sold digital artwork for around $700,000. More specifically, a Generative Adversarial Network (GAN), which imitates human creativity by employing convolutional neural networks, was used to create the portrait. Research *demonstrates that RNNs, or recurrent neural networks, can also be used to create GANs.*

Given a large amount of training data, these GANs can develop into incredibly accurate AI systems because deep learning models often get better over time. GANs have been used to produce "DeepFakes," or lifelike imitation photographs and videos of humans, using enormous clusters of Nvidia GPUs.

Even well-known companies like Nutella are utilising AI extensively for design automation.

According to a Futurism article, 7 million different designs for Nutella jars were produced using AI, and they were all soon sold out. According to MIT Technology Review, businesses today employ AI for product design, from Siemens to Renault.

People's money has spoken loud and clear: AI can draw, and it can draw beautifully.

*Thanks to a model known as **DALL-E 2**, AI has more recently made a true quantum leap in its* *capacity to produce images. The results of this AI, created by OpenAI (a research lab), which can generate visuals from textual descriptions, are, to put it mildly, mind-blowing.*

DALL-E 2, despite being in its early stages, holds a lot of potential for the development of AI picture production. DALL E's initial iteration could only produce 256 by 256-pixel graphics. The resolution has been quadrupled to 1024 by 1024 in the most recent version.

By applying that argument to its logical conclusion, it is simple to picture a day in the future when AI will be able to produce visuals and eventually films that are indistinguishable from reality. The far future may witness AI-generated films that are identical to Hollywood blockbusters when combined with an AI-generated soundtrack.

It's interesting to note that DALL-E functions similarly to OpenAI's language model GPT-3, which can produce text in response to a prompt. However, the model is trained using matrices of RGB values for each individual pixel rather than text.

While AI art used to have a dreamlike, psychedelic character, it is now convincing enough for the human eye. This has broad repercussions for the world of art as well as for industries like advertising and film.

It's not difficult to envision a time in the future when AI art commands a sizable portion of the $65 billion worldwide art market. The public's imagination is being captured by AI art, which was once deemed to be incapable of creativity.

AI composes music

The International Computer Music Conference, the Computing Society Conference, and the International Joint Conference on Artificial Intelligence all cover the topic of artificial intelligence and music (AIM). At Michigan State University, the inaugural International Computer Music Conference (ICMC) took place in 1974. The use of AI in music composition, performance, theory, and digital sound processing is currently being researched.

The creation of music-making software applications that utilise AI is a crucial aspect of this field.

AI in music also simulates cerebral activities, similar to applications in other industries. In computer accompaniment technology, where the AI is capable of listening to a human performer and providing accompaniment, the ability of an AI system to learn based on past data is a major characteristic. Interactive composition technology, in which a computer creates music in reaction to a live performance, is likewise powered by artificial intelligence. There are more AI applications in music that deal with marketing and consumer behaviour in addition to music composition, production, and performance. A number of music player programmes have also been created that use voice recognition and NLP technology for voice control of music.

Industry experts are aware of how onerous the licensing procedure for music can be. **Amper Music** *is a cloud-based platform that makes it easier for users to compose music in a range* *of musical genres, making it ideal for use in generating soundtracks for movies and video games.*

*The **AIVA Technologies** team has been working on creating an AI script that can create moving soundtracks for commercials, video games, and movies ever since the company was created in 2016. Soon after, the AI issued its debut work, Opus 1 for Piano Solo. In the years that followed, AIVA also released an album and wrote the soundtrack for a video game. AIVA can be used to develop variants of already-existing songs in addition to allowing users to compose music entirely from scratch. The AI-powered music composer's music engine eliminates the requirement for music licensing, which greatly simplifies the production of corporate or social media films.*

***Jukedeck startup:** both use neural networks to assess music data and then teach the AI how to make unique music, the AI music composer created by the Jukedeck startup is similar to the one created by Amper. You can edit each track that is offered through this AI music composer, changing its duration or tempo.*

Ecrett music *is an online AI music composer that makes it seem simple to create beautiful soundtracks for movies. To create music for a video, all you need to do is upload the video, choose the scene type, and the mood of the scene. You can select from a variety of scenes, including parties, travel, and fashion, with everything from happy to serious moods.*

Melodrive*: the Indie edition of this AI music composer still has more possibilities, even though both the Lite and Indie versions of Melodrive are currently available for free download. One of the first AI programs that can create original, emotive music in real time is called Melodrive. By adjusting to the media environment, the AI creates music with the goal of capturing the tone and aesthetic of the video. It is important to keep in mind that Melodrive is currently under development and that over time its musical composition abilities will improve even further.*

*With **ORB Composer**, you can't make music on your own because the AI makes music based on your preferences. Because of this, in order to utilise the ORB Composer effectively, you must be familiar with at least the fundamental principles of music creation. Nearly all of the chord progressions used in popular music are included in the extensive collection of chord* *progressions included with the AI music creator. This tool is intended for musicians who are curious about exploring the potential of artificial intelligence in music creation and learning about new musical genres. You can arrange different musical blocks into compositions using any one of the six available music templates.*

Amadeus code: *This iOS-based tool lets both experienced musicians and music lovers quickly and easily create new melodies. The chord progressions for some of the most well-known songs ever written are included in the AI engine that powers the Amadeus Code, and you can utilise them to construct fresh and original musical compositional structures. Furthermore, you can rewrite certain sections of songs you've already written using gestures.*

Humtap *is a great tool for musicians who struggle to recall their own ideas because they can simply hum a melody and the program will instantly create a full song utilizing various instruments. Additionally, rhythms may be added with a single tap, and once the music has been created, you can continue by adding vocals. Humtap also allows you to make videos, so you can do this for any songs you write with this app. You can save any songs or videos produced by the Humtap AI music* *composer to your phone.*

Muzeek *is one of your greatest options if you require licensed music for the video you intend to share on social media platforms. The AI system Muzeek employs analyses the films you're making music for and then generates soundtracks that flawlessly match the beat of the video. Online marketing companies and video game producers alike may rely on Muzeek AI's music composer to provide real music of the highest caliber. Additionally, Muzeek has the ability to analyse the video's original audio and extract subtitles from it or automatically change the loudness.*

Brain.fm: *the main tenet of the Brain.fm platform is the notion that music may increase our brain's productivity. Artificial intelligence is employed by a team of scientists, musicians, and engineers to create music that is intended to increase focus and productivity. They assert that the effects of the music produced by their AI music composer can be felt in as little as ten to fifteen minutes. However, since this platform is better suited for people who spend a lot of time at work and have trouble staying focused while completing crucial tasks, you cannot use Brain.fm to make your own music.*

Because most of these technologies are still in development, the prospects that AI music composers present have not yet been fully explored.

AI-generated literature:

AI systems have been able to generate literature, including poetry and fiction, using natural language processing algorithms. However, it is generally thought that AI-generated literature is limited in its creativity and originality compared to that produced by humans.

AI systems can analyze patterns and structures in language and use them to generate new text that is coherent and follows the rules of grammar. However, the content of the text is often based on pre-defined parameters and lacks the depth and nuance of human-written literature.

AI-generated literature is often used as a tool to assist humans in the writing process, rather than as a replacement for human writers. It may be able to generate ideas or outlines for stories, but it is unlikely to be able to produce literature that is on par with that produced by humans in the near future.

AI-created games:

There are many games that have been developed using AI algorithms, including:

Card games: AI systems have been used to develop card games that can be played against a computer opponent, including blackjack and poker.

AI systems have been utilized to develop a variety of video games, including strategy titles and those that let players control fictitious characters.

Artificial intelligence (AI) technologies have been utilised to develop puzzle games like Sudoku and crosswords.

Games for boards: AI algorithms have been utilised to develop board games like Go and Chess.

AI systems are employed in these games to develop the logic and rules of the game as well as to produce movements or actions for computer-controlled players. AI-generated games are frequently utilised for both enjoyment and testing and refining the capabilities of AI systems.

There is on-going debate about whether AI can be truly creative in the same way that humans are. Some people believe that AI can generate novel ideas and produce original works of art, music, and literature, while others argue that it is limited to working within pre-defined parameters.

On one hand, AI systems have been able to generate art, music, and literature that has been well-received by humans. For example, AI-generated music has been used in film soundtracks and AI-generated art has been exhibited in galleries.

On the other hand, these creations are typically produced using algorithms that have been programmed by humans, and they are based on patterns and structures that have been fed into the system. Some argue that this means that the AI is simply following rules and is not capable of true creativity.

Overall, it seems that AI has the potential to be creative to a certain extent, but it is unlikely to surpass human creativity anytime soon.

CHAPTER EIGHT

FUTURE OF AI

The future of AI is a topic of much speculation and debate. While it is difficult to predict exactly what the future holds, there are a few potential impacts of AI that are worth considering:

Increased automation: *AI has the potential to automate many tasks that are currently performed by humans, leading to a shift in the types of jobs that are available. Some experts predict that AI will lead to widespread job displacement, while others believe that it will create new job opportunities in areas such as data analysis and AI development.*

Improved efficiency: *AI has the potential to significantly improve efficiency in a variety of industries, from healthcare to manufacturing to transportation. For example, AI-powered* *chatbots can handle customer service inquiries around the clock, freeing up human employees to focus on more complex tasks.*

Enhanced decision-making: *AI can analyze vast amounts of data and make decisions based on that data, potentially leading to more accurate and objective decision-making in fields such as finance and healthcare.*

Increased personalization: *AI can be used to personalize products and services to individual users, providing a more tailored and convenient experience.*

Improved quality of life: *AI has the potential to improve quality of life in various ways like assisting with daily tasks: AI-powered devices and systems, such as virtual assistants and smart home systems, can assist with tasks such as scheduling, reminder, and controlling household appliances, which can make daily life more convenient and efficient and providing personalized recommendations: AI has the potential to provide personalized recommendations for products, services, and experiences based on an individual's preferences and history, which could make it easier for people to find what they need and want.*

More intelligent and autonomous systems*: As AI advances, we may see the development of more intelligent and autonomous systems that can perform tasks with minimal human intervention. This could lead to the creation of new industries and the disruption of existing ones.*

Potential for AI to augment human intelligence: *Some experts believe that AI has the potential to augment rather than replace human intelligence, potentially leading to a new era of human-machine collaboration.*

Continued development of AI governance: *As AI becomes more prevalent, there will likely be increased efforts to establish guidelines and regulations for its development and use. This could include measures to ensure the ethical and responsible use of AI, as well as the development of standards and best practices for AI design and deployment.*

Advancements in natural language processing*: AI systems are getting better at understanding and generating human-like language, which could lead to more realistic and engaging virtual assistants and other language-based AI applications.*

Increased use of AI in healthcare: *AI has the potential to transform healthcare by assisting with tasks such as medical image analysis and drug discovery, as well as by providing personalized recommendations for treatment and care.*

AI and the arts: *AI has the potential to revolutionize the arts by allowing for the creation of new types of art and music, as well* *as by providing new tools for artists and musicians to use in their work.*

AI and education: *AI has the potential to transform education by personalizing learning experiences, providing personalized recommendations for coursework, and enabling students to learn at their own pace.*

AI and the environment: *AI has the potential to be used to address environmental challenges, such as climate change and resource depletion, by providing new insights and solutions.*

AI and transportation: *Self-driving vehicles and other AI-powered transportation systems have the potential to transform the way we travel and could lead to significant changes in the transportation industry.*

AI and finance: *AI has the potential to transform the financial industry by enabling more accurate and efficient decision-making, improving risk assessment, and enabling personalized financial recommendations for customers.*

In almost every sector, artificial intelligence is influencing how people will live in the future. It already serves as the primary force behind developing technologies like big data, robotics, and the Internet of Things, and it will continue to do so for the foreseeable future. Some experts predict that AI will lead to significant advances in fields such as healthcare, transportation, and education, while others caution that it could lead to significant disruptions in the job market and raise ethical concerns.

Ultimately, the future potential of AI will depend on how it is developed and used, and it is important for society to consider the potential consequences and implications of this technology as it continues to advance.

CHAPTER NINE

MYTHS SURROUNDING AI

There are many myths surrounding AI, including the idea that it will eventually surpass human intelligence and potentially pose a threat to humanity. While it is important to consider the potential consequences of AI, it is also important to recognize its limitations and the potential it has to augment and enhance human abilities. There are many myths surrounding artificial intelligence (AI), including the following:

AI will eventually surpass human intelligence and potentially pose a threat to humanity: *While it is true that AI has the ability to perform certain tasks more efficiently than humans, it is unlikely that it will surpass* *human intelligence as a whole. AI is not capable of experiencing emotions or creativity in the same way that humans are, and it is unlikely to pose a threat to humanity.*

AI will take over all jobs: *While it is true that AI has the ability to automate certain tasks, it is unlikely that it will completely replace all jobs. In fact, many experts believe that AI has the potential to augment and enhance human abilities, rather than replace them.*

AI is a new technology: *While AI has gained significant attention in recent years, it is actually a field that has been around for decades. The concept of creating intelligent machines dates back to the 1950s, and AI has made significant progress over the years.*

AI is a monolithic entity: *AI is actually a broad term that encompasses a variety of different technologies and approaches. There is not one single "AI" that is capable of performing all tasks, and different types of AI are better suited to different types of tasks.*

AI is always accurate and unbiased: *While AI has the ability to process large amounts of data and make predictions or recommendations, it is not always accurate and can be influenced by the data it is trained on. If the data used to train an AI model is biased, the model will also be biased. It is important to ensure that AI is developed and used in a responsible and ethical manner, and to consider the potential biases and limitations of the technology.*

AI is a magic solution to all problems: *While AI has the potential to solve certain problems more efficiently than humans, it is not a magic solution to all problems. AI is a tool that can be used to augment and enhance human abilities, but it is not a replacement for human creativity and critical thinking.*

AI is not transparent: *While some AI systems can be difficult to understand, it is possible to make AI more transparent and explainable.*

There are various techniques and approaches that can be used to improve the transparency of AI systems, such as explainable AI (XAI) and model interpretability.

AI is not regulated: *While there is currently no comprehensive global regulation of AI, there are various initiatives and organizations working to address the ethical and societal implications of the technology. For example, the European Union has released a set of ethical guidelines for AI, and the United States has established a National Artificial Intelligence Research and Development Strategic Plan.*

AI is only used by large tech companies: *While large tech companies do make extensive use of AI, it is not limited to them. AI is being used in a variety of different industries and sectors, including healthcare, agriculture, finance, and education.*

AI is only used by experts: *While AI does require some technical expertise to develop and use, it is not limited to experts. There are many tools and resources available that make it easier for non-experts to use AI, and it is becoming increasingly accessible to a wider range of users.*

AI is only used for high-level tasks: *While AI can be used to perform high-level tasks such as decision-making and strategy development, it is also being used to automate more routine and mundane tasks. For example, AI can be used to process and analyze large amounts of data, freeing up humans to focus on more complex tasks.*

AI is only used by large organizations: *While AI is being used by large organizations, it is also being used by small and medium-sized businesses. In fact, many smaller organizations are using AI to gain a competitive advantage and improve their operations.*

AI is only used for specific tasks: *While AI is often used for specific tasks such as image or* *speech recognition, it can also be used for more general purposes. For example, AI algorithms can be trained to perform a wide range of tasks by being fed large amounts of data and adjusting their behaviour based on the results. This is known as machine learning.*

AI is only used by humans: *While AI is primarily developed and used by humans, it is also being used by other AI systems. For example, one AI system can be used to train another AI system, or multiple AI systems can work together to perform a task.*

AI is only used for profit: *While it is true that AI has the potential to generate profits for businesses, it is also being used for non-profit and humanitarian purposes. For example, AI is being used to analyze medical data and help to improve patient outcomes, or to optimize the distribution of aid in disaster-affected areas.*

AI is only used by advanced countries: *While AI is being developed and used by advanced* *countries; it is also being developed and used in other parts of the world. In fact, the development of AI is a global phenomenon, and many countries are actively investing in the technology.*

AI is only used by companies: *While AI is being used by companies, it is also being used by governments and other organizations. For example, AI is being used by governments to improve the efficiency of public services and by non-profits to analyze data and improve decision-making.*

AI is only used for high-stakes tasks: *While AI can be used for high-stakes tasks such as decision-making and strategy development, it is also being used for more low-stakes tasks such as customer service and content moderation.*

AI is only used by a few people: *While AI requires some technical expertise to develop* *and use, it is not limited to a small group of people. In fact, there are many tools and resources available that make it easier for a wider range of users to work with AI.*

Conclusion

In conclusion, artificial intelligence has come a long way since its inception, with significant advances and achievements in various fields. From healthcare and science to agriculture and cyber-security, AI has the potential to revolutionize the way we live and work. While AI has the ability to perform complex tasks and make decisions, it is important to recognize that it is still a developing technology and there are limitations to its capabilities.

As we move forward, it will be crucial to continue researching and developing AI in a responsible manner, taking into consideration the ethical and societal implications of this technology. While there are concerns about the potential for job displacement, AI also has the potential to bring about significant positive changes in various sectors.

Looking to the future, it is clear that AI will continue to play an important role in shaping the world we live in. With continued research and development, the potential for AI to bring about positive change is vast.